BORN
TO
EXCEL

BORN TO EXCEL

LIVING A HOPEFUL, MEANINGFUL AND FULFILLED LIFE

CHRISTY O. WILLIAMS

BORN TO EXCEL: Living a Hopeful, Meaningful and Fulfilled Life
Copyright © 2018 by Christy O. Williams
borntoexcel.nbp@gmail.com

Published by New Beginnings Publishing (NBP)

All Scripture quotations, unless otherwise indicated, are taken from the New King James Version®. Copyright © 1982 by Thomas Nelson. Used by permission. All rights reserved.

Scripture quotations marked (AMP) are taken from the Amplified Bible, Copyright © 1954, 1958, 1962, 1964, 1965, 1987 by The Lockman Foundation. Used by permission. www.Lockman.org.

All emphasis in the Scripture quotations are the author's.

Edited by Christine Sopczak
Cover Design and Interior Layout by Steven Plummer

ISBN: 978-0-9940812-0-9

This book is designed to provide information and motivation regarding the subject matter covered. It is sold with the understanding that the author and publisher are not engaged in rendering any type or kind of professional advice. The author and publisher specifically disclaim all claims for damages, including any liability resulting from or incurred from the application or use of the contents of this book.

All rights reserved. No part of this book may be reproduced, stored in a retrieval system, or transmitted in any form or by any means—electronic, mechanical, digital, photocopy, recording, or any other, without the prior permission of the publisher.

Dedication

To my Heavenly Father—thank you for the privilege of writing this book. I am greatly humbled and give You all the glory.

To everyone who wants to live a hopeful, meaningful and fulfilled life… this book is for you.

Contents

	Introduction ix
Chapter 1:	Identity 1
Chapter 2:	The Word 17
Chapter 3:	Prayer......................... 29
Chapter 4:	Self-Acceptance 37
Chapter 5:	Relationship with Parents 51
Chapter 6:	Relationship with Friends 61
Chapter 7:	The Free Gift................... 69
Chapter 8:	The Essential First Step 83
Chapter 9:	The Helper..................... 97
Chapter 10:	Born to Excel................... 107
	Acknowledgements 111
	About the Author 115

Introduction

Some of us experience a hunger or craving, a burning desire to live a more meaningful and fulfilled life only to have past circumstances, fear, confusion, or even our environment, guide us, be the basis of our decisions, and define us. We allow them to determine who we are, how we should live, and who we should become. However, they are not a stable foundation on which to build a life so the hunger and craving continue.

For some of us, life is an experiment as opposed to a journey. It is like driving without a map, directions, or assistance in a country we're visiting for the first time. We get frustrated by our circumstances and wonder what lies ahead.

Some of us wonder about life, some of us are curious about life, and some of us are indifferent about life. We struggle with questions, search for answers, and are assailed by troubling and confusing thoughts:

- I feel there is something missing that I just can't figure out.
- I think I've got it all but I can't help feeling life is pointless.
- I feel confused.
- I feel hopeless.
- I feel discouraged.
- I feel lonely.
- I feel inadequate.
- I feel so overwhelmed with burdens.
- I feel so unfulfilled.

If you are dealing with any of these thoughts or any of the major challenges many people face such as an identity crisis, lack of purpose, rejection, broken or wrong relationships, anxiety, loneliness, sadness, and feelings of hopelessness, then good news! You are in the right place at the right time. This book is about the missing something. It's about dealing with the confusion and struggles so you find the part of you that has been ignored, unknown or undeveloped.

More importantly, this book is to encourage you. My goal is that when you've finished reading this book you will

Introduction

know, for sure, without a doubt, that there is a special plan, place, and purpose for you—that you are important, valuable, special, and your life makes a difference. You can triumph over what might be holding you back, you can live a meaningful life, be fulfilled, and be happy in an unhappy and crazy world.

Now is the time to build yourself up for the journey ahead. It is your era of victory and new beginnings. It is time to create a strong foundation for a purposeful and fulfilled life.

CHAPTER ONE

Identity

One of the most important things in life is self-discovery. Some of the deepest questions we ask ourselves are the following:

- Who am I?
- Where did I come from?
- Why am I here?
- What can I do?
- Where am I going?

These questions are profound because the answers create the framework for our identity, heritage, purpose, potential, and destination. They do not refer to our roles as daughter, son, husband, wife, friend, relative, employee, employer, or member of a group. They do not ask about our ethnic heritage or country of origin. They go beyond those answers. They are the tough questions of life.

Most of these questions are linked—if we do not know who we are (our identity) and where we came from, we cannot know why we are here and where we are going. Knowing our identity is critical. When we do not know who we are, we paralyze our purpose, our potential, and our future.

So how do we find the answers to all the deepest questions about our identity, heritage, purpose, potential, and destination?

Well, let's think about it this way—when we need information about a product, we ask the maker, creator, or the manufacturer. For example, computer programmers create programs and ensure they work well; the programs are then packaged and introduced to the market for customers to buy and install. When we buy the product, we may read an instruction manual provided by the manufacturer. The manufacturer knows the program best and has all the answers about the product. There is a Creator who created us, knows us best and has all the answers to our questions. We did not get to planet earth by some accident. So who created and knows us best? God created us. He packaged us in our mother's womb. He brought us forth through our mothers and introduced us to the world. He knows our identity and our heritage and can help answer the questions we might have.

The Creator (God) wants us to live with complete knowledge of our identity, and to live in the fullness of peace, joy, and fulfilment—not to live in ignorance or fear or with an identity crisis. The Creator wants us to know our identity but to do that, we need to go back to the foundation, the beginning.

The Foundation

Scripture gives the account of the history of creation in Genesis, chapters one and two. In the beginning, God created the heavens and earth. God created the entire universe. He created man to live on the earth and fill it; He created the first man and woman—Adam and Eve—and from Adam's descendants arose the whole human race. Mankind is the pinnacle of all that was created. God created us for connection, fellowship and relationship, and to live beautiful, fulfilled and abundant lives.

Some may ask, "Who is God?" God is God. God is the Creator of the heavens and the earth—the entire universe. God is Self-Existent, All-Sufficient, Sovereign, and Everlasting. God is Love, Holy, Faithful, Righteous, Gracious, and Merciful. God is the Owner of the universe. Before anything was, God existed. God was before the beginning of time. He is now in time, and will be after the end of the world. In other words, God did not begin when the beginning began; He began the beginning—He was before the beginning. He is the Ancient of Days. He is the Living God. He is The Father. He is God Almighty.

God the Creator said:

"...I am the First and I am the Last; Besides Me there is no God (Isaiah 44:6).

Indeed My hand has laid the foundation of the earth, And My right hand has stretched out the heavens; When I call to them, They stand up together (Isaiah 48:13).

I have made the earth, And created man on it. I—My hands—stretched out the heavens, And all their host I have commanded (Isaiah 45:12).

...He who formed you from the womb: 'I am the Lord, who makes all things...' (Isaiah 44:24b, 43:10e).

...Before Me there was no God formed, Nor shall there be after Me" (Isaiah 43:10e).

Amazingly, the universe exists in an incredible balance which God controls and upholds. When we take a look at planet earth, it is impossible to grasp the vastness of the other planets, or the entire universe. Scientists have discovered billions of galaxies with billions of stars in them. God can do with the universe whatever He wants—He created it.

"Whatever the Lord pleases He does, In heaven and in earth, In the seas and in all deep places" (Psalm 135:6). The greatness, the power, the glory and the splendor of everything in heaven and on earth is His. He is perfect in knowledge. His understanding is infinite. His wisdom is profound. His power is vast. He performs wonders that cannot be fathomed.

He says:

> *"...For I am God, and there is no other; I am God, and there is none like Me, Declaring the end from the beginning, And from ancient times things that are not yet done, Saying, 'My counsel shall stand, And I will do all My pleasure" (Isaiah 46:9-10).*

We can never know all there is to know about God. He knows and understands all things—everything about life, everything about the universe, everything about us. Scripture says, *"Have you not known? Have you not heard? The everlasting God, the Lord, The Creator of the ends of the earth, Neither faints nor is weary. His understanding is unsearchable"* (Isaiah 40:28).

Yet, this same God wants us to know that we are the pinnacle of all that He created. Although God created us, the pinnacle of all His creation, circumstances might make us feel otherwise. Just like consumers criticize computer products, people criticize other people and we criticize ourselves. We hear and use terms like inadequate, defective, mistake, slow, unsuitable fit, outdated, unacceptable, failure, or not good enough. This criticism can lead to an identity crisis. We doubt who we are because we are criticized. We see ourselves based on self-condemnation and how other people see us and what they think of us.

God knows our identity, worth, potential, and distinctiveness. God knew every one of us before our conception and birth. He knows who we are, where we came from and for what specific reason and purpose He intended us. He has a deeper knowledge and insight of His creation than the world could possibly see or know because He knows who His creation is (who you are) and what He has put into His creation. His is a product with an established and reputable identity designed to operate according to what He, the Creator, has predestined. Therefore, only the "manufacturer" knows the true identity (as well as purpose and ability) of His creation and has the complete truth. Every other person has opinions.

Opinions do not change our identity, purpose, potential, or destiny but they could delay, divert and/or destroy them—if we allow them. As the One who created us and has complete knowledge of our identity and purpose, let's allow God, who knows us best, help us embrace who we truly are. God says:

"Before I formed you in the womb I knew you... (Jeremiah 1:5a).

Listen to Me,... [you] who have been upheld by Me from birth, Who have been carried from the womb: Even to your old age, I am He, And even to gray hairs I will carry you! I have made, and I will bear; Even I will carry, and will deliver you" (Isaiah 46:3-4).

The Source of Answers

The five questions asked at the beginning of the chapter are answered by the One who created and formed us. We can obtain the answers to these questions from our Creator. Some of us search everywhere for answers but not from God. We try to figure it out on our own. We experiment and try things out based on our circumstances.

When we look to God to find out who we are we will be amazed. God can provide the answers to us in various ways. He can provide the answers through the Word (the Scriptures) and through prayer. He can speak to us directly, He can speak to us through dreams or visions, He can speak to us through our life experiences, and He can speak to us through people.

For example, God spoke directly to Abraham. He called Abraham and told him to leave his country for a land where He would make him father of a great nation. God also spoke directly to Moses to lead the Israelites out of slavery in Egypt to the Promised Land, Canaan. God showed Joseph events about his future through dreams. God spoke to David through Samuel that he (David) would become the king of Israel. Through His angel, God spoke to Samson's mom about Samson before he was born. He told her that the boy would begin to deliver Israel out of the hand of the Philistines. Likewise, before John the Baptist was even conceived, God sent His angel to tell his dad, Zacharias, that John would turn many of the children of Israel to the Lord their God, turn the hearts of the fathers back to the children, to make ready a people prepared for the Lord.

God strategically places amazing people (regardless of their faith, beliefs, and cultural background) in our life to work with us and help us. The same way there are helpers for us, likewise we are helpers to others. God can use whomever He wants. The Creator is the only source for the complete truth about our identity and He can reveal this truth to us however He chooses.

Who Am I?

In the beginning, the Creator, your Creator, our Creator, God said:

Identity

> *"Let Us make man in Our image, according to Our likeness" (Genesis 1:26).*

Each and every one of us was created in the very image and after the superb likeness of God; we are nothing less than the bona fide handiwork of God. Just like products are identified by their makers—they bear the image and name of manufacturers—we bear God's image.

We are also told:

> *"... You are a chosen generation, a royal priesthood..., His own special people, that you may proclaim the praises of Him who called you out of darkness into His marvelous light" (1 Peter 2:9).*

And:

> *"The Spirit Himself bears witness with our spirit that we are children of God, and if children, then heirs—heirs of God and joint heirs with Christ..." (Romans 8:16-17).*

You are a child of God—that's who you are! Our identity, therefore, is found in God, our Creator; our identity is in Christ—if we believe. We are complete in Christ. God wants us to embrace who we truly are (in Him). God looks at what He's created us to be, He looks at our identity in Him and, He looks at who we are in Him. He wants us to know we are His very own. Regardless of our faith, philosophy, background, homeland, skin color, or lifestyle, every person is precious and special to God.

Where did I come from?

As children of God, our heritage is "I am of God." Psalm 127:3 says:

> *"Behold, children are a heritage from the LORD…"*

That's right. We can answer the question "where did I come from?" The Creator said *"Before I formed you in the womb I knew you"* (Jeremiah 1:5a); this tells us that before our birth parents even conceived us, God the Creator knew us. We didn't get here by some cosmic accident. Not only will God care for us and carry us throughout our lifetime, God carried us before we were born—*"Listen to Me,… [you] who have been upheld by Me from birth, Who have been carried from the womb: Even to your old age, I am He, And even to gray hairs I will carry you!…* (Isaiah 46:3-4).

Why am I here?

How do we know the Creator's plans and purpose for us? How do we know the will of God for our life? Why did the Creator put us here? God the Creator said *"For I know the thoughts that I think toward you, says the Lord, thoughts of peace and not of evil, to give you a future and a hope"* (Jeremiah 29:11). We should understand that whatever God makes, He has already known and predestined for good. Manufacturers want their products to do well in the market. God wants us to do well. His design and desire for us is to accomplish the plans He created us for. He wants us to excel, to live a meaningful and fulfilled life. So "why am I here?" The Lord through His apostle Paul says:

> *"... to present your bodies [dedicating all of yourselves, set apart] as a living sacrifice, holy and well-pleasing to God, which is your rational (logical, intelligent) act of worship. And do not be conformed to this world [any longer with its superficial values and customs], but be transformed and progressively changed [as you mature spiritually] by the renewing of your mind [focusing on godly values and ethical attitudes], so that you may prove [for yourselves] what the will of God is, that which is good and acceptable and perfect [in His plan and purpose for you.]" (Romans 12:1-2, AMP).*

If we are determined to know God's plans and will for our life, He will reveal it to us. His plans for us will inspire, motivate, and keep us on track.

What can I do?

We need not worry about our abilities because whatever God made, He's already prepared and equipped. Remember the computer programmer ensures the program works well before it is packaged and put on the market; before we showed up, God knew our abilities and He's confident and very pleased with our abilities, of what He made, of what He's put into His creation. This takes us back to the beginning again. During creation, after God created man, He didn't say "this is good" but "*this is very good.*" He was very pleased. God wants our attitude to be:

> *"I can do all things through Christ who strengthens me" (Philippians 4:13).*

According to the Word, we should believe that we can do all things. The only person who can limit us is us. Therefore, we should not criticize or condemn ourselves. We will never reach our full potential as long as we are against ourselves. Let's not measure God's plans and agenda for our life by our own capacity, thoughts or imagination. In the Word, it is written, *"For My thoughts are not your thoughts,*

Nor are your ways My ways," says the LORD. "For as the heavens are higher than the earth, So are My ways higher than your ways, And My thoughts than your thoughts" (Isaiah 55:8-9). God will surely make us successful in everything we do—if we obey Him (Deuteronomy 30:8). But we cannot just stay idle, be negligent, lazy and expect God to make us successful; we must play our part. God will not do for us what He's already given us the ability to do for ourselves. Even when we feel we're not sure of what the will of God is or even what the next step is and we're asking God and trusting to know His will, we need to remember *"Whatever your hand finds to do, do it with your might"* (Ecclesiastes 9:10a).

Where am I going?

If God is our peace, and we hope and trust in Him, we should try and be hopeful about where we're going. *"For God did not appoint us to wrath, but to obtain salvation through our Lord Jesus Christ"* (1 Thessalonians 5:9). We should tell ourselves *"Surely goodness and mercy shall follow me All the days of my life; And I will dwell in the house of the LORD Forever"* (Psalm 23:6).

I started this chapter by saying "one of the most important things in life is self-discovery." Self-discovery is a journey and while the Scripture passages above help to answer the questions I posed, there is still much to discover. The next chapters provide a map and directions for this journey of self-discovery.

CHAPTER TWO

The Word

Heaven and earth will pass away, but My Words will by no means pass away (Matthew 24:35).

The Creator has a manual for us called Scripture, The Word of God, The Word. It is the manual for our best life. Through the Word, God provides answers to the questions we have. The Word is the Creator's directions, the manual for us to know who we are, where we came from, why we are here, what we can do and where we are going. In the process, we learn to know Him. God uses His Word to answer the profound questions mentioned at the beginning of chapter one.

When we purchase a new cellphone, we find the owner's manual enclosed. It contains information on setup, usage, maintenance, safety, and warranty. Often, we set up the product and start using it without reading the manual. We think we are familiar with the product or a similar device, or we feel we are intelligent enough to get by without reading the manual. We forget the manufacturer knows everything about the product and has outlined what we need to know in the manual. The manufacturer includes knowledge and instructions, "uniqueness and plans," as well as recommendations and solutions, "answers." The manufacturer knows exactly how and what to "enlighten" us on in order to use the phone well. Likewise, the Word is the manual for life. It has all the solutions and answers. It gives us instructions and guidelines for a meaningful and fulfilled life. In addition, in the Word, we find answers on how to handle the challenges of life when they arise. Should we have concerns, the first thing we should do is turn to God, turn to His manual, the Word, to find answers and comfort.

The manufacturer also includes warranty information in the manual. When there are issues, we are expected to look at the warranty section in the manual. The warranty normally states that "if the product is defective or fails to work as expected, do not attempt to fix it yourself. Return it to the manufacturer or take it to an authorized dealer." Why? The manufacturer wants to take responsibility for the product. The Manufacturer (Creator) and Authorized Dealer for us is God. There are, however, lots of unauthorized dealers like confusion, frustration, anger, anxiety, drugs, alcohol, fear, depression, low self-esteem, rejection, loneliness, lust, pride, emptiness, self-pity, self-hatred, bitterness, discouragement, resentment, wrong sex, and unforgiveness; all of these are bad. But the reliable and dependable Manufacturer, God, the

Authorized Dealer, perfectly and completely fixes, restores, and enlightens His own at His own expense. In the Word, He says:

> *"Behold, I am the Lord, the God of all flesh. Is there anything too hard for Me? (Jeremiah 32:27).*
>
> *...I am the Lord your God, Who teaches you to profit, Who leads you by the way you should go"* (Isaiah 48:17).

He has laid out solutions and answers for us in His Word. The Word says, He is "*...the God who holds your breath in His hand and owns all your ways...*" (Daniel 5:23d). In other words, He is the God *"in whose hand is the life of every living thing, And the breath of all mankind?"* (Job 12:10). God is consistent, reliable and dependable and Scripture—the Word of God—is the most consistent, reliable and powerful knowledge there is.

Before we were born and before creation, the Word existed and when heaven and earth pass away, the Word will still exist. The Word is the same today as it was 2000 years ago. There is no modern Scripture, new age Scripture, or Scripture for the new generation. There is only One Word. Times may have changed, but the Word has not changed. God's position has not changed.

The Scripture is a Living Book. It is alive. It is Spiritual. That is how powerful the Word is. It is written:

"For the Word of God is living and powerful, and sharper than any two-edged sword, piercing even to the division of soul and spirit, and of joints and marrow, and is a discerner of the thoughts and intents of the heart" (Hebrews 4:12).

In the Word, God told us everything we need to know to live a triumphant life. We can search the Word to see what is said about us. However, if we approach the Scripture simply as religious text, we will miss out.

The Right Knowledge

Ignorance can be dangerous. Being uninformed can be risky. The opposite of ignorance is knowledge. The Creator said, *"My people are destroyed for lack of knowledge"* (Hosea 4:6a). But *"through knowledge the righteous will be delivered"* (Proverbs 11:9b). It is, however, dangerous to have knowledge that is wrong and untrue; we need the right knowledge and understanding. When we are equipped with truth, knowledge of the Word, we cease to be enslaved; we cease to be victims. In John 8:32, the Word declares that *"And you shall know the truth, and the truth shall make you free."*

We should dig into the manual, the Word to know the truth, to know about ourselves; it helps us become self-aware and informed. It builds our faith. We need to encounter the Word, the right Knowledge—truth.

In order to deepen our understanding, we need to encounter the Word through hearing, reading and meditating. Doing so will help us deal with ignorance. We will receive answers to our questions. As we dig deeper, we gain understanding about ourselves, about life, and about God.

Scripture says *"So then faith comes by hearing, and hearing by the Word of God"* (Romans 10:17). Hearing the Word builds our faith. The message about Christ can be heard through the Word. We will gain knowledge of what we do not know when we are open and receptive to hearing the Word of God, including the Word preached and interpreted by Spirit-filled people blessed and called by God. We will also have a deeper understanding, especially of certain Scripture about which we may need explanation.

God also expects us to read Scriptures, not just listen to what others say. Scripture is not just for others to read and share with us. We should not be satisfied with what we hear from people, at church, watch on television, listen to on the radio, and see on the internet; we need to read the Word and see for ourselves. We need to read the Word so that we can feed our spirit. Also, reading Scriptures helps our human spirit be receptive to sound doctrine preached. On several occasions when the Lord was asked questions by the religious leaders or when He needed to explain or clarify something during His teachings, He said *"Have you not read?"*

At first, it can be overwhelming to read Scriptures. We might feel like it's a lot and we are not sure where to begin. As long as we are willing, the Lord will help us. We do not have to read Scriptures from the beginning or straight through (it does not mean we cannot read the whole text from beginning to end). We can start anywhere. We can continually take small steps to know more of Scriptures. Eventually we may want to read and know as much as we can because as we read the Scriptures we will desire it more and more. We will be amazed and overwhelmed with awe at the power of God, how Almighty He is, who and what He is to us, and who we are to Him. It is mind-blowing. Simply by reading, we feel the power, peace, joy and especially, the love of God.

It is important to understand that we will never be done with Scripture because it is the Living Word of God. We keep learning and growing. We should read continuously as long as we live. The Word is new every day. Even if we have read it before, we can still receive new revelations when we read it again. We will never wake up one day to amazingly discover that we have acquired all the knowledge and answers we need in life. As long as we live, we will always need the Word. For it is written, *"if anyone thinks that he knows anything, he knows nothing yet as he ought to know"* (1 Corinthians 8:2). One of the remarkable things about the Scriptures is that we feel amazing when we read it, understand it, and receive awareness and insights, when we are with God in a quiet, peaceful and relaxed atmosphere.

Carving out time and effort to think and reflect on Scripture, especially as it relates to our personal life or circumstance is important. It is written, *"This Book of the Law shall not depart from your mouth, but you shall meditate in it day and night, that you may observe to do according to all that is written in it. For then you will make your way prosperous, and then you will have good success"* (Joshua 1:8). Thinking and reflecting on the Word brings great benefit to the soul. It helps us apply the Word to our personal life and circumstances.

The more we hear and read the Word, the more we get closer to God, the more we discover ourselves. We will find ourselves becoming familiar with certain verses that address critical questions and areas in our life, and when we reflect on them, we will develop the right attitude and positive outlook toward life. Basing our decisions on the Word of God and His values provides freedom and peace because God's principles, His guidelines for life, are tried and true. The Word gives us confidence and takes away doubts and fears. In His Word, God gave us the answers to the questions we have, but we need to dig (hear, read and meditate) into the Word to deepen our understanding and individually receive revelations from God through His Spirit.

The Importance of Learning for Yourself

It is vital to know for ourselves why we believe what we believe and to have a clear and solid faith. We need to have a good grasp of the Word and we need to get to know God for ourselves. No one can learn for us. Others can't drink to quench our thirst; we have to drink to quench our own thirst. We need to personally know, connect, and experience who God is to us, what He is to us, who we are to Him, and what He has for us. We have to build our own personal conviction.

The Lord does not want the Word to be forced on us but for us to discover truth, to seek the truth, to ask for answers. The choice is ours. In Matthew 7:7, He said *"Ask, and it will be given to you; seek, and you will find; knock, and it will be opened to you."* The Word increases peace in our life and builds our confidence and trust in God. We should go to the Word to learn God's position on everything, especially us. In the world we live in, it is risky not to learn about ourselves, the position of God on the matters of life and the way we should go. The more we acquire the right knowledge, the more we find answers to the questions we have, and the more we become balanced in our thoughts, decisions, attitudes, and actions. Nothing and nobody can mislead or debate us out of that which God has revealed to us.

As for God, His way is perfect; The Word of the LORD is proven; He is a shield to all who trust in Him (Psalm 18:30).

CHAPTER THREE

Prayer

In addition to the Word, one of the greatest keys that God has given us is prayer. God did not create us to figure out life and do life on our own; He did not create us to be by ourselves. He is very much interested in us—our joys, our relationships, our doubts, our concerns, and our disappointments. Prayer is talking and listening to God. It is through prayer that we communicate with God. It is through prayer that we make our requests known to God and obtain what we need. It is through prayer that we intercede for others. It is also through prayer that we ask God to tell us about our identity, spiritual heritage, purpose, potential, and future.

Sometimes we become anxious, discouraged, confused or frustrated because we have not called on our Creator; we have not talked to God, we have not listened to what He has to say to us. We have not prayed. God says:

"Call to Me, and I will answer you, and show you great and mighty things, which you do not know" (Jeremiah 33:3).

God encourages us to call to Him—to reach out—through prayer, even when we are confused, afraid or worried. Paul the Apostle said *"Be anxious for nothing, but in everything by prayer and supplication, with thanksgiving, let your requests be made known to God"* (Philippians 4:6). If we are willing, if we are receptive, God can show us great and mighty things. He can tell us remarkable secrets. He can inspire us. He can give us great and amazing ideas, ideas that impact lives positively. The more we pray, the more we get closer to God and the more we discover.

Prayer is us giving God permission to interfere in our affairs. It is also God giving us permission to interfere in our divine assignments—our divine affairs. We sometimes think that it is up to God to do something about our concerns. The truth is we need to participate in the solution and we participate in the solution through prayer. God is just waiting for us to talk to Him and to ask Him for help. Remember He said, *"Behold, I am the LORD, the God of all flesh. Is there anything too hard for Me?"* (Jeremiah 32:27). Nothing is hard for God.

How to Pray

Some of us, however, may have never prayed and may need to learn how to pray; the Lord, in His Word, taught us how. He said:

> *"... When you pray, go into your room, and when you have shut your door, pray to your Father who is in the secret place; and your Father who sees in secret will reward you openly. And when you pray, do not use vain repetitions...*
>
> *...For your Father knows the things you have need of before you ask Him. In this manner, therefore, pray:*
>
> *Our Father in heaven,*
> *Hallowed be Your name.*
> *Your kingdom come.*
> *Your will be done*
> *On earth as it is in heaven.*
> *Give us this day our daily bread.*
> *And forgive us our debts,*
> *As we forgive our debtors.*
> *And do not lead us into temptation,*
> *But deliver us from the evil one.*

For Yours is the kingdom and the power and the glory forever. Amen" (Matthew 6:6-13).

With time and through consistent communication with God, we will improve our prayer life. We will learn to talk more to Him, learn what to ask and pray more. The beauty about praying to God is that God knows what we need before we even call to Him. So we need not feel pressured as we learn to communicate with God.

Prayer is a Necessity

Daily, consistent conversation with God is vital. Prayer is not an option; it is a necessity. Prayer is a tool we need in our everyday life. Through prayer, we ask God to guide us, protect us and help us. Through prayer, we can tell God to use us to help people in need. Through prayer, we can remain steadfast and confident that with God's help and promise in His Word, we can do all things and be fulfilled. Even when confusion, doubt, concern or discouragement tries to set in, or when there are detours, through prayer we can ask God for clarity, peace, strength, favour, and direction. Through prayer, God encourages us and restores our hope, peace and trust in Him.

Sometimes, a crisis may overwhelm us, but we need to pray through challenging periods, because God is the only Person who can perfectly give us the support and love to take us through the rough seasons. God reminds us that challenges are temporary.

Maybe we are going through a difficult or challenging period—we should not stop communicating with God or stray. We should continue to pray. In Luke 18:1-8, the Lord told a parable to encourage us to always pray and never give up. We should make an effort to thank, worship, and praise God, even if we don't feel like it. This is where our strength and victory lie. If we are worried that we've got a long way to go, through prayer, we can tell God that we are thankful for hope in Him.

If life seems not to be working out, it does not mean that God does not answer prayers or that God has changed. God is unchangeable. He remains the same, *"If we are faithless, He remains faithful..."* (2 Timothy 2:13). He will always be with us. He says:

> *"Fear not, for I am with you; Be not dismayed, for I am your God. I will strengthen you, Yes, I will help you, I will uphold you with My righteous right hand" (Isaiah 41:10).*

Prayer is not just about asking for something or seeking only answers for our life but also about thanking and appreciating God—and letting Him know how much we love Him.

Through prayer, we let God know, that regardless of challenges, we know He remains a Good, Loving, Kind, Gracious and Merciful God. So instead of looking at how far we have to go, let's look back and thank God for how far He's already brought us. Instead of focusing on the challenges and allowing them to overwhelm us, let's focus on His promises. Instead of looking at what we do not have, we should tell Him how thankful we are for what we have—if we think we have nothing, we should thank God for what we hope for. If we feel there is nothing to hope for, we should thank God that we are alive. Therefore, instead of dwelling on an issue, we should dwell on His mercy and promises. We have no idea of all the things God does behind the scenes on our behalf for our good (some of which we will never know). We must learn to remain confident in God regardless of the situation, continue to communicate with Him, and learn to give thanks to Him at all times.

We can learn to talk and listen to God and live one day at a time as we continue on the journey of self-discovery; we should choose to be happy, live each day enjoying what we have right now, and be thankful for the blessings of each day. We need to always interact with God through prayer to help us live a happy and fulfilled life. We can count on God to take our prayers and use them to bring blessings to us and to others. Our prayers make a difference.

CHAPTER FOUR

Self-Acceptance

The value that we put into who we are and "Whose" we are matters; our value rests in God and nothing or no one else. Complete value and acceptance can only come from our Creator who knows and loves us better than we love ourselves and better than anyone else loves us. Our self-image connects with how much acceptance and respect we have for ourselves.

Self-acceptance can be difficult because of self-condemnation and rejection by others. However, we can either choose a life of gratitude and happiness or a life filled with doubt, regret, shame, guilt, condemnation, and low self-esteem. Only we can make ourselves "inferior or cheap." Nobody else can.

Self-Condemnation

We know what self-rejection looks and sounds like. We condemn and criticize ourselves. We feel sorry for ourselves.

Self-condemnation is believing the negative opinions and ideas that we have about ourselves.

Self-condemnation or self-rejection are problems most of us have faced at some time. If not dealt with, they can become lifelong struggles. We dislike and reject ourselves, we are anxious about being rejected, and we compare ourselves to others.

If we are not secure with ourselves, how can we accept ourselves for who we are and who God wants us to be? The truth is God knows what we are made of and what He designed us for. Let me explain. God custom-made us just the way He wants us. He determines the uniqueness of our attributes, personalities, and abilities. If we judge God's creation, that is, condemn and reject ourselves, we are criticizing God. Scripture says, "*...who are you to reply against God? Will the thing formed say to Him who formed it, "Why have You made me like this?"* (Romans 9:20). It is written, "*It is He who has made us, and not we ourselves*" (Psalm 100:3b). Therefore, we should have nothing—I mean absolutely nothing—to be ashamed of.

God does not see our physical appearances or circumstances. He sees us in His image and after His likeness. From the very beginning of creation, God declared that He will make us in His image and after His very Own likeness. The Word says "*So God created man in His own image*"

(Genesis 1:27a). This means that we have been created just as the Creator wanted. The Word also says after the fifth day of creation, when God had created everything, apart from human beings, He was pleased "...*And God saw that it was good*" (Genesis 1:25c), but on the sixth day, after He created human beings, Scripture says He was very pleased. "*Then God saw everything that He had made, and indeed it was very good*" (Genesis 1:31). Therefore, God is not just pleased with how He created us; He is very pleased. We are made in God's image, of His beauty, excellence, glory, and splendor. We are uniquely made by God. Therefore, do not demean or discredit what God created in His image, what He's very pleased with, and of course, what He values and has accepted—you. Self-condemnation and self-rejection are not needed.

Rejection by Others

Rejection by others can negatively affect our self-acceptance also. Often, instead of accepting ourselves based on how God values us, we base our acceptance on what other people think of us.

We do not need other people's approval to feel good about ourselves or to feel valuable. Otherwise, we will continually look to or rely on them for affirmation. The negative words and attitudes of people cannot affect our self-worth unless we permit them. Everybody is not going to like or accept us, and that's okay. Refuse to feel bad, down, or disappointed. If some people do not accept us, it may be God's way of protecting us from harmful influences and relationships. He knows the end of everything.

We do not have to check in with other people or wait to see what they do or say before we do something, go somewhere, say something, wear something, relate to someone, or feel a certain way. We should not let anybody determine how we should feel about ourselves. With God, we are accepted and important without anyone's approval.

So How Can We Accept Ourselves?

- Accept the love of God
- Develop right thinking
- Accept and love yourself

Accept the Love of God

First and foremost, we have to accept the love of God. We can surround ourselves with many people yet still feel unloved, insecure, rejected, and lonely. Only by accepting the love of God can we truly feel accepted, valued, loved and free of loneliness. God is love and the love of God is available for us all, but many have refused to accept it or may not be aware of it. We need to accept God's love and always remember that we do not have to work to merit the love of God. In fact, there is nothing we can do or will do to make God love us any less. Nothing will separate us from His love or change the love He has for us. In Jeremiah 31:3, God says:

> "... Yes, I have loved you with an everlasting love; Therefore with lovingkindness I have drawn you."

In Romans 8:35, 38-39, Apostle Paul said:

> "Who shall separate us from the love of Christ?... For I am persuaded that neither death nor life, nor angels nor principalities nor powers, nor things present nor things to come, nor height nor depth, nor any other created thing, shall be able to separate us from the love of God which is in Christ Jesus our Lord."

Human love can grow weak or cease to exist but not God's love. Also, there could be rejection after acceptance—people can change their minds; not so with God. He never changes. His acceptance and love are consistent and unconditional. God loves us because of who He is. God is Love.

Even though God may not like some things we do or say

and He may not like the lifestyle some of us have chosen, that does not mean He hates or has rejected us. He dislikes the wrongdoings, not the person. Even when we displease Him, He will not stop loving us. When we displease Him, He wants us to confess our wrongdoings to Him and ask for forgiveness. God will forgive us many, many, many, many, many, many, many....... times (Psalm 86:5, 1 John 1:9). He is a Merciful and Gracious Father. We do not lose His love, kindness and mercy. God said *"For the mountains shall depart And the hills be removed, But My kindness shall not depart from you, Nor shall My covenant of peace be removed, Says the Lord, who has mercy on you"* (Isaiah 54:10).

The love of God the Father is incredible!

It is great to be loved by your dad (earthly dad)! You feel special and protected. He provides the best he can for you and makes you feel valued and cherished. No earthly dad, however, values and loves his child or children more than God loves His children. No earthly dad desires to do more and better for his children than what our Heavenly Father— Daddy God does. We should be amazed at what we have in God, how special and valued we are to Him and how much He loves us. When I think about it, it's difficult to grasp.

Another marvelous point to know is that God knows and loves each of us individually. His love is personal. It is written, *"the very hairs of your head are all numbered. Do not fear therefore; you are of more value than many sparrows"* (Luke 12:7).

So how do we accept the love of God the Father? Through a relationship with Him and His Son, Christ. The more we get to know God, the more we embrace His love for us and the more we love Him and then, of course, the more we feel valuable and accept ourselves.

Develop Right Thinking

After we accept God's love, we have to choose our thoughts and attitude. We have to develop right thinking and focus our mind on the positive.

To change the way we see and feel about ourselves, we must change our thinking through the Word (with the help of the Holy Spirit). The Word shows the Lord's way of thinking and how He wants us to think. By dwelling and meditating on the Word and believing what the Word says about us, we will see that our value and acceptance do not depend on our physical appearance, background, intellect, social status, age, education, bank accounts, automobiles, home, or what others think. When we realize this, then we can have the right thoughts and learn to accept ourselves. The Word produces right thinking, and right thinking leads to right feelings, so in essence, we are what we think.

Our actions should align with what we think and what we say so we have a positive mentality. We should learn to avoid certain words and ignore certain thoughts. The fact that a negative thought comes to mind does not mean we must entertain and nurture it. Likewise, we should not entertain or reflect on the negative things we hear from others. Whenever possible, try and avoid negativity and criticism. We need to avoid negative thoughts (and people) that bring us and others down. We must learn to always *"cast down arguments and every high thing that exalts itself against the knowledge of God, bringing every thought into captivity to the obedience of Christ"* (2 Corinthians 10:5). Paul pointed out a strategy for right thinking. He said:

> *"...whatever things are true, whatever things are noble, whatever things are just, whatever things are pure, whatever things are lovely, whatever things are of good report, if there is any virtue and if there is anything praiseworthy—meditate on these things" (Philippians 4:8).*

The major obstacle to right thinking is conforming to the patterns of this world. Romans 12:2a says, *"And do not be conformed to this world, but be transformed by the renewing of your mind..."* We need to be vigilant and careful, and learn to know when to ignore certain information, ideologies and behaviors. So much is going on right now around the world that it is hard for people to keep up. We can be at home yet connected to the whole world. The change and improvement in technology is good but at the same time it can be detrimental. All sorts of ideas, philosophies, images, and opinions are shared on television, the internet, magazines and radio and it is up to us to filter out the garbage. We have the choice of getting the good out of it or letting it pollute our thoughts and our mentality. Moreover, we are in control of our hands, eyes, the remote and the mouse. They are not in control of us. Know when to change channels, turn off the TV, turn off the radio, leave a website, or close the browser. There are sites on the internet we should never even consider going to. And if we stumble on something that is not edifying, we need not take a second look or spend another second of our precious time on it.

Also, there are books, articles, magazines, and journals we should not read. We will pollute our eyes and minds. The Lord said, *"The lamp of the body is the eye. Therefore, when your eye is good, your whole body also is full of light. But when your eye is bad, your body also is full of darkness"* (Luke 11:34). We should not take in whatever is given to us. We do not have to conform to the patterns of the world—we are in the world, but not of the world. Believing the bad opinions and ideas we read or see can lead to us feeling poorly about ourselves and not accepting who we are.

It is written, *"Keep your heart with all diligence, For out of it spring the issues of life"* (Proverbs 4:23). Guarding our eyes and what goes into our heart in a confused and crazy culture or society is challenging and yet this is crucial to developing right thinking and fundamental to self-acceptance; it requires courage, self-discipline, determination and a big dose of the grace of God. We can ask God to help us with the distractions of our mind and eradicate foolish thoughts that will interrupt our thinking process so that we can learn to accept ourselves for who we are.

Accept and Love yourself

Once we embrace the Father's love and develop right thinking, we can develop a healthy self-love and concept of ourselves. We begin by accepting and loving ourselves.

We can accept ourselves because we have divine value and dignity. Our worth before God is measured by His love for us, which is unconditional. He wants us to see ourselves as loved and lovely.

We should not want to or try to be like other people. In fact, why would we want to be someone else? Why must we have what they have? Why must we look like someone else? Why would we want to be lost in someone else's identity?

Also, we don't have to live our lives trying to prove something to other people. We should not compare ourselves with others. It's okay to admire, appreciate, and celebrate others, but not if it means we do not accept ourselves.

We cannot give or show real love to others if we don't love ourselves. Always remember that God custom-made you just the way He wants you. You should see yourself as God's masterpiece, His very own special possession, estimably valued and dear to Him. Therefore, like you. Be happy with you. Celebrate yourself. Learn to spend time with yourself. It's okay to take yourself out and very okay to go on vacation by yourself and have a good time—if you need to. Accept and love yourself (in a healthy way). You should confidently say:

> *"I will praise You, for I am fearfully and wonderfully made; Marvelous are Your works, And that my soul knows very well" (Psalm 139:14).*

See Yourself as God Sees You

Self-acceptance is a result of seeing yourself as God sees you. Tell yourself that you would rather be you than anybody else on the face of the earth. Be nice to yourself. Take good care of yourself. Appreciate yourself. You are excellently, wonderfully, beautifully, and uniquely made by God, the

Creator of the entire universe. He makes no mistakes. He is the One who knows you (inside and out) better than any person on earth. He is the One who accepts you perfectly. He knows and wants the best of the best for you—for each and every one of us. See yourself as you truly are—a person of priceless value. Let no one tell you otherwise. This is not pride or arrogance; it is confidence in God. No one can take away your value. See yourself as a worthwhile person, created by God, redeemed by God, and precious to God. In Him you are fully accepted, unique, special, and complete!

CHAPTER FIVE

Relationship with Parents

RELATIONSHIPS ARE NECESSARY and important. Relationships can make our life richer. We cannot live our life without relationships. Through relationships, God can bless, care, encourage, comfort, and love us. Through relationships, God can speak to us. Through relationships, God can help us fulfil our destiny. We should appreciate and enjoy being with people because we get to see and sense the One whom we love in other people. Relationships, however, impact our life and are our futures. Understanding why and how they do is crucial so we can learn to develop the right relationships based on God's love for us and the people we are in relationships with. Aside from our relationship with God and with ourselves, there are several relationships that can influence us but a major relationship to look at is our relationship with our parents. Scripture say:

> *"Behold, children are a heritage from the Lord,*
> *The fruit of the womb is a reward.*
> *Happy is the man who has his quiver full of them;*
> *They shall not be ashamed..." (Psalm 127:3, 5).*

Children are gifts from God! We are valuable assets. We shouldn't see ourselves as an inconvenience. We are rewards to our parents when we grace their lives.

One of the greatest blessings any child can have is to have parents who love and fear God. God asks parents to bring up children in the way they should go. When we have parents who invested in us, who brought us up in the way of the Lord, who instilled and developed the right values and mindset in us, we have been saved a lot of time and energy.

I know there are differences in upbringings; there are some of us who have or have had good relationships with our parent(s). Also, some of us have had or still have difficult or strained relationships with our parent(s) and may still be struggling with terrible and awful childhood experiences. Some of us may have been emotionally, physically, sexually, or psychologically abused. Also, some of us may have an amazing and great dad but not mom and vice versa. Some of us resent our dad because of the way he treated our mom or resent mom because of how she treated dad, while some of us were abandoned or ignored by one or both parents. Some of us may have (or had) very controlling parents(s)—who try to make us take certain steps or make certain decisions, not minding if they are pleasing to God but for their own personal interest. And I know there are parents who were and still are remarkable.

Some parents compromise and even deprive themselves to ensure that the needs of their child or children are met. Some have sleepless nights thinking about the well-being and future of their children. They shower their children with love, care and support even when they are unruly. Some are so kind and thoughtful that before they make certain decisions, they consider the impact they will have on their children. They put the emotional state, the consequences, and the future of their children before selfish interests or personal gain.

Our relationship with our parents is mentioned in Scripture:

> *"Children, obey your parents in the Lord, for this is right. 'Honor your father and mother,' which is the first commandment with promise: "that it may be well with you and you may live long on the earth"" (Ephesians 6:1–3).*

Some people struggle with the above Scripture, perhaps because of what parents said, what they did, or what they were or are involved in. Some people had, and may still have, difficult or broken relationships with their parents. The pain may still be devastating for some, which may have contributed to self-condemnation and rejection. Some people struggle with honoring their parents. Unfortunately, nothing can change the past. What we can do is allow God to change how we feel about what happened or what is still happening. We can ask God to help us.

Turn it Over to God

Some parents may realize their wrong deeds and apologize. But what if they never come around and just refuse to accept or own up to their wrongdoings, or even stop them? Should we live the rest of our life in resentment and unforgiveness? Certainly not! With God's help, we can still forgive. We can let go for our emotional and spiritual health. We can allow God to help us. He can give us the grace to forgive. If parents ever realize, own up and ask for our forgiveness, nice. If not, then we have already forgiven them and long since moved on.

Unforgiveness is like poison in our body. Know that if we hold anything against our parents or anyone it hinders our prayers, our blessings and our relationship with God. It may even affect our relationships with others. It's not worth it.

It is written, *"whenever you stand praying, if you have anything against anyone, forgive him, that your Father in heaven may also forgive you your trespasses"* (Mark 11:25). Forgive for your sake, not their sake. Forgiveness is a choice, but we can forgive as an act of obedience to God.

If our parents are still involved in things clearly contrary to God's ways, we still need to forgive. Try not to dwell on those things but continue to pray for them. However, in certain situations, we can forgive but it might be better to avoid them. It may be in our best interest to keep our space. We must be careful to ensure they do not get us involved or influence us to do or support anything that displeases God or conflicts with the Word of God. If it is helpful, we should communicate with our parents, respectfully and honorably to let them know how we feel.

Appreciate

If we have great parents, we should appreciate them and thank God every single day for such a wonderful blessing. It might not be both parents, even if it is just mom or just dad who has been there for us, let's still appreciate them. It is a great blessing to have parents who fear and obey God, who follow the will of God and who are willing to be there for us!

Also, some amazing parents who do not have a relationship with the Lord or believe in God, by nature, do things that are right, kind and thoughtful; they instill morals and values in their children. Some of these parents are regarded as heroes by their children. So let's appreciate our parents and respect their input, opinions and experience—that please God. It is written:

> *"A fool despises his father's instruction, But he who receives correction is prudent (Proverbs 15:5).*
>
> *A wise son makes a glad father, But a foolish son is the grief of his mother" (Proverbs 10:1).*

You Are Not Alone

Some people may say "well, I do not know what you are talking about. I do not have and never had anyone to call parents. I was abandoned. I was rejected. I was given up for adoption. I never had a stable home..." They feel hurt and bitter. Perhaps they have wondered over the years why their parents did not want them, why they came into this world in the first place, why they were given up for adoption, or why they lived in foster homes.

Our birth parents may not have planned us, but God did. I know this will be hard to believe but it does not matter what situation we find ourselves in, or the circumstances of our birth. Neither does it matter what we have been told nor what we have seen or experienced; we are legitimate children. We were not born by mistake—we're no accident or misfortune. We are gifts from God. We should not let anyone or any circumstance make us feel or think otherwise. We are blessings from God, not burdens, not liabilities. We were already conceived in the mind of God long before we were conceived by our birth parents. According to Isaiah 43:1, our Creator who formed us said He called us by name. He ransomed us. We are His very own. God our Father also says:

> *"Listen to Me, ... [you] who have been upheld by Me from birth, Who have been carried from the womb: Even to your old age, I am He, And even to gray hairs I will carry you! I have made, and I will bear; Even I will carry, and will deliver you (Isaiah 46:3–4).*
>
> *I will not leave you orphans; I will come to you"* (John 14:18).

This is beautiful. Our Heavenly Father said He carried us before we were born and will be our Father, our God throughout our lifetime. So, regardless of the circumstances of our birth, our genealogy is "I am of God" which answers the question of "Where did I come from?" I cannot emphasize how important it is for us to acknowledge and hold onto God as our Father. It is very important that we know and believe how present God is to us as our Father and that He is indeed undeniably our Father.

If we have a great relationship with our parent(s), we should always appreciate them and take their (good, godly) instructions and corrections seriously. If we had or still have an unpleasant relationship with one or both of our parents, we need to believe, allow and trust God to heal our broken hearts. Nothing is impossible with God.

CHAPTER SIX

Relationship with Friends

In addition to our relationship with our parents, another major relationship is with our friends. It is good to have friends. We can celebrate together, confide in each other, and support each other when the need arises. We do life together. Friendships are some of the most valuable relationships we have.

We are influenced by our friendships; this influence will either be good or bad depending on the values, characters, and beliefs of our friends. The kind of people we spend time with will, to a large extent, determine our life's direction. Our success can be smothered by our mindset, culture, environment, and even, at times, our friends. Our choice of friends can lead to pleasure and success or calamity and devastation, so we need to be careful with whom we relate and those we allow to influence us. A true friend, the right friend, will not cause us problems and will not lead us to destruction. But some friendships are toxic. As much as friendship is amazing, relationships are necessary, and we should enjoy being with people, we are better off with no friends than to have the wrong kind of friends.

The Danger of Bad Friends

Keeping a close relationship with someone who will lead us astray or negatively influence us and especially our relationship with God is risky. When we hang around bad friends, their ways may rub off on us if we are not careful. Certain people we hang out with make us feel drained and down afterwards. This is not to say that we are better than them or that we are perfect. This is about us not falling or being negatively influenced. Even though we disagree with all or most of their values, ideas, and behavior, if they are the stronger influence, they can sway us. No matter how good an egg is, if we mix it with a bad egg we will have a bad omelet. The bad influence is always stronger. Scripture says:

> *"Do not be deceived: 'Evil company corrupts good habits' (1 Corinthians 15:33).*
>
> *He who walks with wise men will be wise, But the companion of fools will be destroyed" (Proverbs 13:20).*

Associating with people who possess negative outlooks on life and negative attitudes about themselves and others is dangerous. These are the people who constantly complain and condemn. They like nothing and see nothing good in themselves and in others. They don't appreciate people. Yet they want to be like everybody else and copy everything they do. They see nothing to be grateful to God for in life. If we remain in their company, their negative attitudes can rob us of the positive mentality and outlook we are trying to build because the more we hang around them, the more we begin to think and act like them.

Friends can also influence us in other ways. Sometimes, we are faced with challenges too complex for us to handle; we may not feel comfortable turning to our parents or other people around us and we may not be knowledgeable about seeking God or turning to Him. Instead, we turn to our friends and if these friends are a bad influence, they might give us the wrong advice that could lead to disaster. Scripture says that Amnon, the son of David, had a very crafty friend whose name was Jonadab; Jonadab gave Amnon bad advice that eventually led to Amnon's death. Who we hang around with, talk to, listen to or confide in, especially when we are most vulnerable, matters a lot. It is written, *"Blessed is the man who walks not in the counsel of the ungodly..."* (Psalm 1:1a). Some advice can derail us if we are not around people who give us godly, wise and honest advice. *"...Can the blind lead the blind? Shall they not both fall into the ditch?"* (Luke 6:39).

We should evaluate the people we hang around with and the friends we confide in. If we notice something scripturally inappropriate, we need to try, at least, to point it out and encourage our friends to choose what is appropriate and also share with them how important it is for us not to displease the Lord. What we view as appropriate may not be what our friends view as appropriate. We do not need to condemn, despise, or criticize them either. Be respectful even though they don't agree with what we agree to. Do not try to fix or change others; only God can do that. But if a friend continues to act in a way that is unscriptural, we might have to make a decision for our own benefit. I know and understand that curtailing relationships or ending them can be challenging, but it is for our own good when the relationships are toxic.

Genuine, Good and Close Friends

Having and keeping true, good, close friendships is essential. Every genuine friendship must be one of shared core values and beliefs; otherwise, it will be a struggle to relate on a deep level. Shared values and beliefs is key because the friendship will be more healthy and fulfilling. The relationship must be one that is adding to us and we are adding to it, and one that does not erode values.

With genuine friends, we explore the deep thoughts of our hearts, our dreams, and our desires. We have the freedom to correct and build each other, *"As iron sharpens iron, so a man sharpens the countenance of his friend"* (Proverbs 27:17). We understand and share our values and our walk with God. We are equally yoked. We may not necessarily have the same plans or purpose, but we have our foundation in Christ and have the desire to please and serve God. We can help and encourage each other.

True friends will accept us for who we are. With true friends, we don't hide struggles. We don't pretend. We are transparent. We feel safe to be vulnerable. We are able to share deep and private things without worrying that they will end up on the internet!

We can have lots of friends and yet be profoundly lonely but not so with the right friends. It feels so good when we hang out with good friends. We should be with people we can learn from and respect. We should be with the right people so that even when we are influenced, it will be for good. There will be times our faith wavers or we're overwhelmed with feelings of concern or inadequacy; a true friend will encourage and build us up at such times. With genuine friends, when something critical arises and we need to ask questions or seek advice, we are surrounded by the right individuals.

Let me tell you, it's such a blessing when we have reliable and genuine friends! They support, encourage and motivate us. The right friends caution us and tell us what we need to hear, not what we want to hear. When we ask them for their opinion, with love they give us genuine affirmations as well as honest constructive criticism. They help us remain grounded in both good and tough times. They give us serenity. Be thankful if you have the right friends and healthy relationships.

Moreover, it's not just about having genuine and close friends, but also about being one. God can help our friends through us.

God strategically puts people in every season of our life. By the same token, we may have been strategically placed in other people's lives to encourage, motivate, love, and support them. Some people, who respect and admire us, will want to learn from us and would like to be motivated positively, so do not avoid them or push them away. The key is that it's not about us; it's not about our qualities, personality, or capabilities. It's about God in us, about God who refined us, who restored us and who is still at work in us!

If you do not have any genuine close friends, that's okay; ask God to bring them into your life and, at the same time, ask Him to help you be a genuine friend to others. However, be cautious and mindful of the people you allow to be close friends. Remember, we are better off with no friends than to have the wrong kind of friends.

CHAPTER SEVEN

The Free Gift

The kingdom of heaven is like treasure hidden in a field, which a man found and hid; and for joy over it he goes and sells all that he has and buys that field (Matthew 13:44).

God is strategic; He sees the big picture for our life, the long-term goals and the end results. We do not have to do life on our own. Why would we want to live life without the Creator who knows it all? He wants us to do life with Him. He wants us to live a meaningful and fulfilled life. We are not here to observe life. He's given us the free gift of salvation (redemption, deliverance from the power and consequences of wrongdoings), and all we need do is receive it.

There's so much going on in this world that can make people feel sad; yes, life may not be perfect, but with God we can start to enjoy where we are now. There is no need and no time to point accusing fingers or blame anyone. Likewise, there is no need for any pain or regret about the past. God says, *"Do not remember the former things, Or ponder the things of the past. Listen carefully, I am about to do a new thing…"* (Isaiah 43:18-19a, AMP).

We cannot deny the fact that sometimes life has its challenges, but that is not to say we must go through life from one challenge to another. We can certainly live a peaceful life and enjoy all aspects of life. God told David that his son, Solomon, "...*shall be a man of rest; and I will give him rest from all his enemies all around. His name shall be Solomon, for I will give peace and quietness to Israel in his days*" (1 Chronicles 22:9). Several years later, after David had passed on, Solomon said "...*now the Lord my God has given me rest on every side; there is neither adversary nor evil occurrence*" (1 Kings 5:4). With God, we can live a peaceful, joyful, meaningful, beautiful, abundant and fulfilled life. Challenges may come, but to stand strong at such times on our own, without God, is torture and misery. We do not have to. The Lord assured us that when trouble comes, He will take care of us and has, in fact, already overcome the troubles. We can hold unto God and His promises. With Him, we come into a place of grace, peace, and victory. He fights for us. He helps us triumph.

To have peace in the midst of the storm, to have God fight for us and take care of us, to receive all-round peace and rest, to fully experience God's blessings, to fully answer the self-discovery questions, to deal with rejection, condemnation, loneliness and broken relationships, to properly and fully use the gifts God has given us, to fill the void in our life, to connect and have a personal relationship with God, and to come into His Kingdom, we must be saved, restored, redeemed—reconciled to Him.

Let me put it this way. Our identity is in God, in Christ, but to claim and live with that identity in Christ, we have to be saved. To walk with God and follow His will for our lives, and to have hope in where we are going (our destination), we have to be saved. To receive understanding and revelations from the Word—His Word, we have to be redeemed. To confidently and securely embrace our worth and value in God, to receive the love of God (by having a relationship with Him, with Christ), we have to be redeemed. To feel and call God our Father, we have to be restored. To figure out that missing something, and to not just enjoy life but to enjoy life to the max and feel fulfilled, we have to be restored.

We might say what does it mean to be saved, redeemed or restored? Why do we have to be saved, redeemed or restored? To understand, we have to go back to the beginning, back to creation. This is necessary because of where we're going next.

The Fall and the Grace Through the Redemption

In the beginning, after God made the earth and everything in it, He turned it over to Adam. Adam was living in harmony and happiness with God. He was living a life of abundance. God gave him dominion over the earth so Adam was responsible for creation. He was expected to obey God's instructions and have trust in God. But the enemy, satan, the devil who hates mankind, did not want mankind to live according to God's amazing plan. satan's mission statement is to "steal, kill, and destroy" so he carried out a deceitful scheme and deceived Eve. He lied to Eve. She believed him, encouraged Adam, and they disobeyed God. Unfortunately, Adam committed high treason and sold out his dominion to the adversary—the enemy, the devil!

Afterwards, the Lord God said to the enemy:

> *"And I will put enmity Between you and the woman, And between your seed and her Seed; He shall bruise your head, And you shall bruise His heel" (Genesis 3:15).*

The immediate aftermath of the fall of Adam (the fall) was a spiritual death—separation—from God and from the Kingdom of God. God is Spirit (John 4:24a). Man is a living being; he has a soul, he has a spirit and he lives in a body. The spirit of man is that part of us which can know God, relate to God, and receive from Him. But Adam and Eve turned away from God and the fellowship with God was broken. There was a spiritual separation. God's presence that guaranteed constant communication left Adam when Adam disobeyed God. God sent Adam away from His presence. The separation led to misery and hardship for mankind and a sense of emptiness.

The consequence of the broken fellowship with God is that we are separated from God and deserve punishment for our sins; now all people, all of us, are born with a sinful nature, *"for all have sinned and fall short of the glory of God"* (Romans 3:23). Restitution was needed to reconnect mankind to God. Mankind needed a restored, reconciled relationship with God; we needed to be redeemed, to be saved. This is where Jesus Christ comes in. Out of God's unfailing love for us, God the Father sent His only Son, Jesus Christ to restore us, to take the punishment we deserve in order to provide salvation:

> *"Being justified freely by His grace through the redemption that is in Christ Jesus, whom God set forth as a propitiation by His blood, through faith, to demonstrate His righteousness, because in His forbearance God had passed over the sins that were previously committed, to demonstrate at the present time His righteousness, that He might be just and the justifier of the one who has faith in Jesus (Romans 3:24-26).*

> *Therefore, as through one man's offense judgment came to all men, resulting in condemnation, even so through one Man's righteous act the free gift came to all men, resulting in justification of life. For as by one man's disobedience many were made sinners, so also by one Man's obedience many will be made righteous (Romans 5:18-19).*
>
> *For as in Adam all die, even so in Christ all shall be made alive" (1 Corinthians 15:22).*

Jesus Christ is our link to connect with God, receive from God, and be in sync with Him. Jesus Christ bridges the gap between us and God the Father. He came to destroy the work of the devil. Jesus Christ, the Saviour came that we may have life, and have it more abundantly—life in all its fullness. Understanding who Christ is, why He came, where He is, and what He is today is extremely vital.

For hundreds of years, the prophets foretold the coming of the Messiah, the Saviour, the Son of the Most High—Jesus Christ. John the Baptist described Him in Mark 1:7 as *"One... whose sandal strap I am not worthy to stoop down and loose."* God spoke to prophet Isaiah concerning the Messiah, who God announced as the Son of God (see Isaiah 9:6-7).

The Arrival

When the fullness of the time had come, God sent His Son, the Messiah, the King, Jesus Christ:

"For it pleased the Father that in Him all the fullness should dwell, and by Him to reconcile all things to Himself, by Him… (Colossians 1:19-20a).

In the beginning was the Word, and the Word was with God, and the Word was God. He was in the beginning with God. All things were made through Him, and without Him nothing was made that was made. In Him was life, and the life was the Light of men (John 1:1-4).

And the Word became flesh and dwelt among us, and we beheld His glory, the glory as of the only begotten of the Father, full of grace and truth (John 1:14).

Yet for us there is one God, the Father, of whom are all things, and we for Him; and one Lord Jesus Christ, through whom are all things, and through whom we live" (1 Corinthians 8:6).

God sent Jesus Christ to reconcile us to Himself. The Word existed before creation, Jesus Christ is the Living Word.

It's all about Jesus Christ!

Jesus is the Christ, the Son of the Living God. God the Father sent Jesus Christ to restore us; you see, He didn't have to do that. Even though He is and always will be the Supreme and Living God of the universe, He did because of His love for all of us. He wants to be in relationship with us! Jesus Christ didn't have to leave heaven to come to earth either, but He did because of His love for us and His desire for us to connect with our Heavenly Father and be in relationship with Him. Jesus Christ is the way God can restore us back to His original intent—back to our original status and rightful place of authority and dominion. Jesus Christ is the way to enter the Kingdom of God. As well, through Jesus, we have eternal life. Jesus Christ, the King of kings is the way to God the Father. That's why Jesus Christ said:

> *"…I am the way, the truth, and the life. No one comes to the Father except through Me" (John 14:6).*

In John 18:37, He said:

> *" …You say rightly that I am a King. For this cause I was born, and for this cause I have come*

into the world, that I should bear witness to the truth. Everyone who is of the truth hears My voice."

He also said:

"For I have not spoken on My own authority; but the Father who sent Me gave Me a command, what I should say and what I should speak. And I know that His command is everlasting life. Therefore, whatever I speak, just as the Father has told Me, so I speak" (John 12:49-50).

Jesus Christ came for all. No matter our beliefs, ancestry, upbringing, lifestyle, birth place, genetic or physical traits, or nation, God wants us to experience His mercy, love, grace, forgiveness, blessings, and relationship. He wants us to be whole. We can claim and have this relationship and experience when we choose to believe and accept Jesus Christ as the Saviour who has made possible a new relationship between God and mankind.

Jesus Christ said:

"For I have come down from heaven, not to do My own will, but the will of Him who sent Me (John 6:38).

...He who believes in Me, believes not in Me but in Him who sent Me.... for I did not come to judge the world but to save the world (John 12:44, 47).

All authority has been given to Me in heaven and on earth" (Matthew 28:18).

And God the Father says:

"This is My beloved Son, in whom I am well pleased. Hear Him!" (Matthew 17:5c).

The Lord Jesus Christ, the Son of God, is the bridge for us to have a direct one-on-one relationship with God, the Father and be whole. The core of our identity depends on our personal relationship with God, with Jesus Christ.

This is not about religion but about spirituality and relationship. It is about having a personal relationship and connection with the Living God. We do not need people or religion to get to God, the Father; we need Jesus Christ.

Mankind's greatest need is a timeless one. Man searches to fill a deep spiritual vacuum, void, and craving of the soul. We search for meaning and fulfilment in life. This search is the search for God and a personal relationship with God. Only God can fill the vacuum. Living without God is spiritual death. We need the help of the Lord to live life—to live a delightful, meaningful, abundant and fulfilled life. We need Christ the Lord. He is Life Himself, the Light of the world. No level of wealth, education, fame, prestige, or accomplishments can connect us to God or measure up to our spiritual connection to God. With Him, we can enjoy life to the max.

To be restored, to have a relationship with God now and forever, to claim and accept all that Christ did on our behalf, and to receive and experience the amazing free gift of God, salvation, we have to take the essential first step.

CHAPTER EIGHT

The Essential First Step

Today, when people talk about a blissful life and enjoying life to the max, they talk about an abundance of material possessions, wealth, position, prestige, achievements, fame and pleasure; these are not bad at all, but they are the least of enjoying life to the max here on earth. We can have earthly abundance and yet remain unfulfilled. The Word says *"...one's life does not consist in the abundance of the things he possesses"* (Luke 12:15b). Of what use are material possessions or wealth, prestige, fame, or positions without grace—unconditional love, mercy, without inner peace, joy, forgiveness, fulfilment and wholeness? These are just some of the spiritual blessings we can receive when we have a relationship with God. God wants our soul to be safe and secure. He wants us to enjoy life completely. He wants us to live a meaningful and fulfilled life. God can help us achieve this if we're humble and willing to take the essential first step.

Christ came down from heaven to be the ultimate sacrifice once and forever to save us! Now *"...we have such a High Priest, who is seated at the right hand of the throne of the Majesty in the heavens"* (Hebrews 8:1) who also makes intercession for us. God clearly told us the conditions by which we can receive the salvation Christ offers. God says we must repent (have a change of direction) and believe (trust Christ to remove our guilt and the penalty of all our wrongdoings). The Word of God says *"...Repent, and believe in the gospel"* (Mark 1:15). Jesus Christ said it plainly; in order to come into the Kingdom of God *"we must be born again"* (John 3:1-8, 13-17). Romans 10:9-10 explains what needs to be done to be born again: *"if you confess with your mouth the Lord Jesus and believe in your heart that God has raised Him from the dead, you will be saved. For with the heart one believes unto righteousness, and with the mouth confession is made unto salvation."* Therefore, being born again—being saved and deciding to receive the free gift of salvation—is the essential first step.

We can choose to have a new beginning. Our Heavenly Father wants us to run to Him, not from Him. He does not expect us to clean up our act first and be righteous on our own before He'll love and save us. We do not clean ourselves up to come to God; we come just as we are and He cleans us up.

The Essential First Step

God wants to heal us. He wants to help us. He wants us to know that we've got what it takes. He wants us to excel, and He wants us to feel unconditionally loved. He wants us to experience life-changing peace, joy, and satisfaction. But it has to be our choice. I made this choice. I took this step and have no regrets. It's been such a privilege. Jesus Christ is incredible!

If you want a personal relationship with God, if you want a new beginning, if you want to accept Jesus Christ as your Lord, if you want to be born again you can make the choice, take the essential first step and say this simple prayer:

"My God, I repent of my sins. Lord Jesus Christ, come into my life. I confess with my mouth the Lord Jesus and I believe in my heart that God has raised You from the dead. I receive You into my life as my Lord and Saviour. Amen."

Beautiful! You have taken the most important step of your whole new life. You've been saved—restored—redeemed. Jesus is now Lord over your life. God is not just God to you anymore; He is God your Father. You are a child of the Most High God. *"But as many as received Him, to them He gave the right to become children of God, to those who believe in His name: who were born, not of blood, nor of the will of the flesh, nor of the will of man, but of God"* (John 1:12-13).

It is a privilege and a blessing to be a child of God, the Creator of the entire universe Who marked off the earth's dimensions. He shakes the earth from its place and its foundations tremble. He speaks to the sun and it does not shine. He seals off the light of the stars. He alone stretches out the heavens and treads on the waves of the sea. He gives orders to the morning and shows the dawn its place. He has entered the storehouses of the snow and has seen the storehouses of the hail. He says to the snow, "*fall on the earth.*" He is excellent in power. He is abundant in mercy and love. He, God Almighty, is your Father, our Father—our God. In His unconditional love, He has chosen to call us His own. There is no greater love.

After the First Step

It is impossible to really become a child of God and not experience change in life. You can talk to the Father, ask Him anything—make your request, relate to Him anytime and anywhere directly. Jesus Christ said:

> "*...Most assuredly, I say to you, whatever you ask the Father in My name He will give you. Until now you have asked nothing in My name. Ask, and you will receive, that your joy may be full*" (John 16:23-24).

The Essential First Step

The Father handles all the needs of our life. Watch Him work! If we are His children, He is personally committed, involved, and mindful of our happiness, health, welfare, peace, joy—all aspects of our life. *"For the Lord will not forsake His people, for His great name's sake, because it has pleased the Lord to make you His people"* (1 Samuel 12:22).

We may still experience temptations; we may stumble. 1 John 1:8, says *"If we say that we have no sin, we deceive ourselves, and the truth is not in us,"* but when we displease the Father, when we sin, as His children, we have the benefit of going back to Him to acknowledge and confess our sins and ask for His forgiveness. He said *"If we confess our sins, He is faithful and just to forgive us our sins and to cleanse us from all unrighteousness"* (1 John 1:9). He will forgive us many, many, many, many, many, many, many times; *"where sin abounded, grace abounded much more"* (Romans 5:20b). He is abundant in grace.

The fact that we displeased the Father does not change our identity in Him and does not mean we are no longer saved; we still remain His children. He wants us to repent from the sin, refrain from repeating it (with the help of our Lord Jesus because we cannot do it on our own) and move on. However, this should not give us an excuse to keep displeasing Him:

> *"What shall we say then? Shall we continue in sin that grace may abound? Certainly not! How shall we who died to sin live any longer in it? Or do you not know that as many of us as were baptized into Christ Jesus were baptized into His death? Therefore we were buried with Him through baptism into death, that just as Christ was raised from the dead by the glory of the Father, even so we also should walk in newness of life.*
>
> *…knowing this, that our old man was crucified with Him, that the body of sin might be done away with, that we should no longer be slaves of sin. For he who has died has been freed from sin. …Reckon yourselves to be dead indeed to sin, but alive to God in Christ Jesus our Lord.*
>
> *For sin shall not have dominion over you, for you are not under law but under grace" (Romans 6:1-4, 6-7, 11, 14).*

Now we see not only what we were saved from, but what we were saved to, a life of freedom, service, purpose and grace.

Our Armour for the Journey Ahead

Life does not automatically become easy after the first step has been made. We may experience trials and challenges, but

Christ the Lord clearly promised to take care of us completely at all times. He clearly assured us that He's got us. He is our defense and refuge.

We need to be strong in the Lord. We need to:

> *"Put on the whole armor of God, that you may be able to stand against the wiles of the devil. For we do not wrestle against flesh and blood, but against principalities, against powers, against the rulers of the darkness of this age, against spiritual hosts of wickedness in the heavenly places. Therefore take up the whole armor of God, that you may be able to withstand in the evil day, and having done all, to stand" (Ephesians 6:11-13).*

Our Father has a plan for our lives. The enemy has a plan too. But the Lord has given us the tools necessary for a victorious Christian life; the full armor of God—truth, righteousness, peace, faith, salvation, the Word of God, and prayer.

Now that we are saved, the Father is saying, hear My Word, read the Manual, the Word, to acquire knowledge, to know My precepts and My commands and to have a better quality of life. Practice what I have laid there. Pray. Abide in Christ. You are not alone. You will be helped. We need to read the Word to know the promises, privileges, benefits, blessings, and especially the precepts and commands of God's Word.

Jesus our Lord pointed out the two greatest commands:

> *"And you shall love the Lord your God with all your heart, with all your soul, with all your mind, and with all your strength. This is the first commandment. And the second, like it, is this: 'You shall love your neighbor as yourself.' There is no other commandment greater than these"* (Mark 12:30-31).

There are spiritual rules and spiritual principles of God that when we apply them, we are doing so for our good.

With the help of God, we can experience His blessings and our soul can be safe and secure with Him. We can live a hopeful, more meaningful and fulfilled life. The Lord can help us because we have taken the essential first step.

The Declaration – Encouraging yourself in the Lord

Taking the essential first step and saying the prayer earlier in the chapter is just the beginning of the journey. As mentioned earlier, reading the Word of God, praying, putting on God's armour and abiding in Christ are very important. In addition, saying—declaring—the following aloud will help us remember who we are, how we are valued and loved by

God and how He wants us to be hopeful and happy regardless of circumstances. Declaring these words (especially during trying times) will encourage us and help reinforce the precepts and promises of God. We should say them as often as we can until they become part of our mindset:

> *"Through Jesus Christ I have right standing with God. I've been restored. I am redeemed. I am saved. I am justified by Christ. I am born again. My citizenship is in heaven. I am a partaker of all heaven's spiritual blessings.*
>
> *I am what the Word of God says I am. I was created in the image and according to the likeness of God, Creator of the heavens and earth. I am a chosen generation, a royal priesthood, God's own special person. My identity is in Christ. I am a child of God!*
>
> *I am of God. I am a heritage from Him.*
>
> *The thoughts and plans of the Lord for me are of peace, to give me a future and a hope. May the eyes of my understanding be enlightened to know God's perfect will, plans, and purpose for my life and the hope He's given me. God knows what is best for me.*

Now, I renounce and loose myself from all negativity, including negative patterns and strongholds. Whoever the Son has set free is free indeed, that means, I am free! Therefore, I align myself to God's original purpose, thoughts, plans, and will for my life.

I can do all things, not some, but all things through Christ who strengthens me. The LORD my God will make me succeed in all works of my hand. And may the LORD rejoice over me for good.

I am special and valuable in the sight of God. Yes! God loves me with an everlasting love. Nothing shall separate me from the love of God which is in Christ Jesus my Lord. I am of more value than many sparrows.

I like me. I appreciate me. I'd rather be me than anybody else on the face of the earth. I am unique. God has accepted me perfectly and completely. I will praise You oh Lord my God, for I am fearfully and wonderfully made; Marvelous are Your works, And that my soul knows well.

I am the temple of God! Greater is Jesus Christ that dwells in me than the enemy that is in the world. Through Jesus Christ I have right standing with God. I refuse to be broken, confused, depressed, anxious, or fearful. I refuse to be a picture of failure. I am an overcomer because I am born of God. No weapon that is formed against me shall prosper. My God will strengthen me. He will help me. Even to my old age and to gray hairs, my Father will carry me; He made me! He will bear me and be with me every step of the way.

Daddy God has crowned me with glory and honour; He will not withhold any good thing from me; every good and perfect gift is from Him. And every blessing of the LORD enriches with no sorrow added to it. By His grace, I will advance. I will bear fruit and I shall continually live in good health because Jesus Christ Himself took every infirmity and bore every sickness. May the Good Lord give me rest, peace and joy on every side.

More importantly, may God help me to love Him and love people.

I ask that the Holy Spirit and Word I have spoken begin to transform me to the original image and intent God designed and purposed me to be. I was

Born to Excel. It is well with me. Surely goodness and mercy shall follow me all the days of my life and I will dwell in the house of the LORD forever.

I declare all these in the name of Jesus Christ. Amen!"

CHAPTER NINE

The Helper

WE CANNOT CARRY on as believers with just our own knowledge, understanding, wisdom, or power. We need the Father to help us. We need Jesus to help us live and enjoy life. It is impossible to do it apart from God—apart from "the Helper." I cannot imagine life without my Father! God has been my Father, Protector, Strength, Provider, Defender, Healer, Friend... He has shown me endless and immeasurable love, mercy, grace and help much more than I deserve. My Lord Jesus is the Champion of my heart and my life. He's been my Comforter, Counsellor, Advocate, Guide and Helper. We need God every single day and we need the help of the Helper—the Holy Spirit:

> "... 'Not by might nor by power, but by My Spirit,' Says the Lord..." (Zachariah 4:6).

The Holy Spirit gives a new experience of God's presence and power. The Holy Spirit is the Spirit of God. God is our Father, Jesus Christ is our Lord, and the Holy Spirit is our Comforter, Advocate, Guide, Counselor, and Helper. A powerful revelation was shown at the baptism of Jesus Christ in the Jordan River (Matthew 3:16-17). Jesus comes up out of the water, the Spirit descends on Him like a dove, and the Father speaks. *"For there are Three that bear witness in heaven: the Father, the Word, and the Holy Spirit; and these Three are One"* (1 John 5:7).

During the earthly ministry of Jesus Christ, before His crucifixion, at the last supper, He promised another Helper from the Father Who would establish a special relationship that was originally and always intended between us and God. He said:

> *"If you love Me, keep My commandments. And I will pray the Father, and He will give you another Helper, that He may abide with you forever—the Spirit of truth, whom the world cannot receive, because it neither sees Him nor knows Him; but you know Him, for He dwells with you and will be in you (John 14:15-17).*
>
> *But the Helper, the Holy Spirit, whom the Father will send in My name, He will teach you all things, and bring to your remembrance all things that I said to you (John 14:26).*

However, when He, the Spirit of truth, has come, He will guide you into all truth; for He will not speak on His own authority, but whatever He hears He will speak; and He will tell you things to come. He will glorify Me, for He will take of what is Mine and declare it to you. All things that the Father has are Mine. Therefore I said that He will take of Mine and declare it to you" (John 16:13–15).

In the beginning, when God created and formed man, He "*breathed into his nostrils the breath of life; and man became a living being*" (Genesis 2:7). The Gospel of John records Jesus doing something similar to His disciples after His resurrection. He said to them "*… As the Father has sent Me, I also send you."* And when He had said this, He breathed on them and said, "*Receive the Holy Spirit*" (John 20:21-22). As He breathed into them they received the Holy Spirit.

We received the Holy Spirit the moment we received Christ. The moment we put our hope, trust, and total dependence in Christ, the Spirit of God came to live in our heart. He lives within us. That means, when we accepted Jesus Christ as Lord and Saviour, when we were born again, our spirits reconnected with God (there was a spiritual disconnection after the fall); the Holy Spirit now dwells with us—lives in us. Spiritually, He lives in all who have received Christ:

> *"... The Spirit of truth, whom the world cannot receive, because it neither sees Him nor knows Him; but you know Him, for He dwells with you and will be in you (John 14:17).*
>
> *In Him you also trusted, after you heard the word of truth, the gospel of your salvation; in whom also, having believed, you were sealed with the Holy Spirit of promise" (Ephesians 1:13).*

When we receive the Holy Spirit, we have Christ in us. We have God in us (John 14:17, John 14:20). We should understand that wherever we go and whatever we do, we are the temple of God (1 Corinthians 6:19-20). We are heavenly royalty—we have the Lord Himself within us. Christ does not reduce Himself to our standards when He comes to live in us; no, rather, He lifts us up to His standards. We must refuse to compromise God's standards. There is never any regret or shame when we set our standards and make decisions based on the Word of God and when we allow His Spirit to guide us.

The Holy Spirit guides us into all truth. As we build our individual relationship with God by investing time in His

Word, through prayer and obedience, the Holy Spirit guides and teaches us who we are, why we are here, what we can do, and where we are going. He tells us what is to come. He helps us embrace our worth and value. He counsels us on our relationships. He teaches and helps us switch our attitudes from the approach of "never enough" to "more than enough" so that we learn to believe not what our eyes see but what the Word of God says.

The Spirit of God guides us along the right path and nudges us to carry out God's will for our life. He helps us to receive revelations from God. As believers, we need to know the mind of God. The Holy Spirit makes known to us that which is in heaven. He takes the things of Christ, declares them to us and makes them real in our life:

> *"...For the Spirit searches all things, yes, the deep things of God. For what man knows the things of a man except the spirit of the man which is in him? Even so no one knows the things of God except the Spirit of God. Now we have received, not the spirit of the world, but the Spirit who is from God, that we might know the things that have been freely given to us by God" (1 Corinthians 2:10–12).*

The Holy Spirit can give us the counsel, wisdom and guidance we need. As it is written, *"I will put My Spirit within you and cause you to walk in My statutes, and you will keep My judgments and do them"* (Ezekiel 36:27). He is the Power that God gives us to carry out the tasks that He inspires us to take on.

Taking the first step by being born again takes place instantly but learning, progress, and transformation is a process. They are continuous and can take a lifetime. When we accept Jesus as Lord, our spirits are made new but still dwelling in an old mindset. Therefore, it is necessary to undergo a change of mindset—a change in our knowledge and thoughts. Our brains need reprogramming with new knowledge about the new us; the Spirit of God will help. Some of us have spent so long with the old knowledge, beliefs, thoughts, ideas, and values, that there are a lot of new things to know and learn. Some of us may even need a complete mental reversal; the Spirit of God will help. He will help us develop the right thinking pattern to transform us.

In order to develop the right thinking pattern and transformation, we need good understanding when we hear and read the Word; it is the Spirit of God that brings that understanding. He helps us understand when we hear and read the Scriptures and helps us remember what we have heard and read. In regard to the Holy Spirit, the Lord said, *"…He will teach you all things, and bring to your remembrance all things that I said to you"* (John 14:26). He will help us in everything.

Living a victorious life without the help of Holy Spirit is very difficult. We need the help of the Holy Spirit to transform us so that we can become more like Christ and let Him change our heart, desires, motives, attitudes and lives so we become compassionate and forgiving, and we love God and one another. He opens our eyes, ears, hearts and understanding so that we can see people and situations through His eyes and truly be able to love one another.

Even though we fully embrace the truth that we are children of God, that our identity is in Christ, and that we are unconditionally loved, accepted and valued by God, there are times when our confidence is shaken because of our own judgement, circumstances, or someone else's words or attitude. There are also times when the struggles, thoughts, doubts, and challenges (mentioned in the introduction of this book) we dealt with, at times, still creep in. It is the Holy Spirit who reminds us we are who God says we are and can give us back our confidence. It is the Holy Spirit who reminds us we are treasured, and we are complete in God. It is also the Holy Spirit who reminds us we are not alone. We're reminded that we are overcomers. It's also in times like these, we can say aloud the declaration outlined in the previous chapter to encourage us. Hearing these words will help reinforce the love of God, His promises, and who we are in Christ.

The Holy Spirit is the best Comforter, Counsellor, and Support we can ever imagine. What gets us through tough times when there is no one and nowhere to go to, when we have no strength to carry on, and we have no idea of what to do? The Comforter, the Spirit of God, gets us through. He helps us in our weaknesses. He strengthens and comforts us. The Holy Spirit is always with us but He becomes more real in difficult times. There are times that, even if we have family and close friends, we may feel that the only Person we want to talk to, listen to, and even be with is God. No greater comfort and peace can there be than to have His presence.

We need the help of the Helper to walk with God, to teach us all things, to give us understanding, to embrace our true identity and worth, to inspire us, and to transform us. The Holy Spirit is here to guide us into all truth and to help us in every aspect of our life.

CHAPTER TEN

Born to Excel

Hear, my son [child], and receive my sayings, And the years of your life will be many. I have taught you in the way of wisdom; I have led you in right paths. When you walk, your steps will not be hindered, And when you run, you will not stumble (Proverbs 4:10-12).

As you have read in this book, God can help us find answers to the thoughts and questions we struggle with. It is through God that we know who we are, where we came from, why we are here, what we can do and where we are going. It is through God that we can have healthy relationships with family and friends. It is through being reborn and accepting Jesus as our Lord and Saviour, having a personal relationship with God and by praying and reading the Word that the void in our life can be filled and we can learn to accept ourselves for who are—children of God.

God has an exclusive plan and purpose for each of us, and He gives each of us special grace to live our life accordingly. Regardless of our detours and dilemmas and no matter how many times we are faced with trials, God still works out all things to conform to His plans, thoughts, and purpose for our life and for our good.

With God, perseverance, determination, and resilience, we will triumph. Therefore, we must look to the future with optimism, focus, and confidence in God because hope, confidence and trust in God never disappoints. God is more than enough to provide all we will ever need. *"He who did not spare His own Son, but delivered Him up for us all, how shall He not with Him also freely give us all things?"* (Romans 8:32).

As we progress through the journey of life, we have to remain connected to God so that He can help us and reveal each phase of the journey and be with us every step of the way. That means when we complete a phase, He reveals, prepares and helps us take the next step.

We might not always understand but we can believe, obey and trust God.

We say, "why me?" He says, *"it is My will. "*

We say, "I'm not altogether yet." He says, *"You don't have to be."*

We say, it's not what I want." He says, *"it's what you need."*

We say, "I can't do it." He says, *"You can do all things."*

You are a victor by virtue of your identity in Christ and heritage in God. You were born to live a meaningful and fulfilled life. You were born to enjoy the best God has in mind for you in all areas of your life.

You were Born to Excel.

Acknowledgements

To my family, I'm grateful to have you as family.

To my editor, Christine Sopczak, thank you for allowing God to use you as the editor of *Born to Excel*. Your expertise and professionalism are second to none. I cherish all the amazing time spent with you.

To Elizabeth Anderson, who encouraged me during this project, thank you!

To my book designer, Steven Plummer, a gifted and an accomplished book designer who is absolutely fantastic to work with, thank you!

To all the wonderful beta readers, thank you for your time, commitment and valuable feedback. I appreciate you. May God fully reward you all!

About the Author

In today's world, where so many are hurting and broken, Christy O. Williams loves to provide hope and encouragement. Christy is an accounting and finance professional and entrepreneur living in Canada and recognizes the value of lifelong learning.

www.ingramcontent.com/pod-product-compliance
Lightning Source LLC
Chambersburg PA
CBHW050435010526
44118CB00013B/1538